The Business Side of Marriage 2.0

Scott J. Spivey

Copyright © 2025 Scott J. Spivey

All rights reserved

The characters and events portrayed in this book are fictitious. Any similarity to real persons, living or dead, is coincidental and not intended by the author.

No part of this book may be reproduced, or stored in a retrieval system, or transmitted in any form or by any means, electronic, mechanical, photocopying, recording, or otherwise, without express written permission of the publisher.

Printed in the United States of America

Preface

Honoring the Past, Embracing the Future

In 2007, Dr. C. Willard Spivey, Jr., Ph.D., and Karon Spivey published *The Business Side of Marriage*, a groundbreaking guide for couples navigating the intersection of love and practicality. Rooted in their decades of experience and research, the book empowered readers to approach marriage not just as a union of hearts but as a financial partnership built on trust, teamwork, and careful planning.

Married since 1959, my parents have lived their philosophy. Through six decades together, they have built a life defined by mutual respect, shared goals, and unwavering commitment. Now living back in their home areas of Manatee and Sarasota counties, their enduring partnership is a testament to the principles they championed in their work.

Why Their Work Matters Today

When my parents first conceived their book, they recognized a glaring gap: couples were often unprepared for the financial realities of marriage. They wanted to change that. By combining actionable advice, relatable anecdotes, and practical tools, they offered readers a roadmap to avoid the pitfalls that derail so many relationships.

Their work was timely and prescient. They tackled issues like budgeting, document management, and long-term planning with the clarity and foresight of true visionaries. But they also left room for adaptation—an acknowledgment that the world, and marriage itself, evolves with each generation.

Carrying the Torch Forward

Now, nearly two decades later, I am honored to continue their legacy. *The Business Side of Marriage 2.0* builds upon their wisdom, bridging timeless principles with modern challenges. It addresses the seismic shifts that have reshaped relationships since 2007: digital transformation, same-gender marriage equality, the gig economy, and the growing role of AI in personal and financial planning.

This book is not just a tribute; it's a conversation with my parents' work. It carries their voice while introducing new tools and perspectives, ensuring that their guidance remains relevant for today's couples. Whether you're a newlywed embarking on a life together, a seasoned couple navigating transitions, or part of a military or first responder family balancing unique demands, this book is for you.

As I step into their footsteps, I do so with gratitude—for their wisdom, their vision, and their belief in the power of marriage as a partnership. This is their legacy, reimagined for a new era.

Transition: A Bridge Between Generations

To further honor their vision, I've included a passage from their original introduction, a timeless reflection on the essence of marriage as a partnership:

"A marriage is a contract between two individuals and represents the formation of a partnership. A marriage has the same requirements as a small business partnership in that the partners combine their assets, liabilities, and incomes to form a successful working system. The way a couple deals with present and future finances will play a key role in their relationship."

—*Dr. C. Willard Spivey, Jr., and Karon Spivey, The Business Side of Marriage (2007)*

Their words remain as relevant today as they were then. While marriage may be rooted in emotion, its success is often shaped by the practical. It requires thoughtful planning, teamwork, and an ability to adapt—qualities that my parents embodied both in their own lives and in their work.

This second edition not only preserves their insights but also expands upon them, addressing the rapidly changing landscape of relationships and financial planning in today's world.

Contents

Preface: Honoring the Past, Embracing the Future

Chapter 1: The Partnership of Marriage

Opening: Welcome to Your Next Adventure

Marriage as Your Joint Startup

The Marriage Business Plan

Case Study: Emma and David

Modern Tools for Modern Couples

Your First Financial Goal

Chapter 2: Building Your Financial Foundation

Opening: The Blueprint for Success

Legal and Practical Preparations

Special Note for Military and First Responders:

Setting Up Financial Systems

Automating Your Finances

Building Your Emergency Fund

Preparing for the Unexpected

Insurance Essentials

Real-Life Example:

Activity: Your Financial Foundation Checklist

Conclusion: A Strong Start

Chapter 3: Creating a Marriage Business Plan

Opening: Charting Your Path Together

Setting Shared Goals

Budgeting for Success

Incorporating Shared Values into Financial Goals

Case Study: Maria and James

Military and First Responders: Leveraging Your Benefits

Activity: Building Your Marriage Business Plan

Conclusion: From Vision to Reality

Chapter 4: Managing Everyday Finances

Opening: Turning Plans Into Action

Banking Basics: Choosing the Right Solutions

Shared vs. Individual Accounts

Credit and Debt Management

Budgeting for Everyday Life

Balancing Fixed and Variable Costs

Managing Emergencies and Unexpected Costs

Housing Costs

Unexpected Expenses

Activity: Managing Day-to-Day Finances

Conclusion: Building Financial Resilience

Chapter 5: Building Long-Term Security

Opening: Planning for Tomorrow, Today

Retirement Planning for Couples

AI Assistance for Retirement Planning

Investing: Growing Your Wealth Together

AI Tools for Investment Insights

Activity: Your First Investment Plan

Protecting Your Partnership: Insurance Essentials

Case Study: Lisa and Mark's Holistic Approach

Legacy Planning: Creating a Lasting Impact

Activity: Planning Your Financial Future

Conclusion: Securing Your Future Together

Chapter 6: Major Life Milestones

Opening: Preparing for the Big Moments
Buying a Home Together
Hidden Costs of Homeownership
Starting a Family
Adoption and Fostering
Career Changes or Business Ventures
Starting a Business
Insurance: Beyond Basic Coverage
Case Study: Maya and Chris
Activity: Your Milestone Checklist
Conclusion: Celebrating the Journey

Chapter 7: Adapting to Challenges

Opening: Strength Through Resilience
Navigating Financial Stress
Creating a Financial Recovery Plan
Coping with Job Loss or Income Reductions
Exploring New Income Streams
Managing Medical Emergencies
Negotiating Medical Bills
Overcoming Economic Downturns
Case Study: Anna and David
Activity: Your Resilience Plan
Conclusion: Facing Challenges as a Team

Chapter 8: Dissolution—Planning for the Unexpected

Opening: Preparing for Life's Difficult Transitions
Divorce: Legal and Financial Steps

Understanding Asset Division

Managing Shared Accounts and Debts

Planning for the Death of a Partner

Managing Life Insurance and Survivor Benefits

Special Note for Military and First Responders

Rebuilding Financial Stability After Dissolution

Rebuilding Savings

Exploring Resources

Case Study: Navigating Life's Transitions

Conclusion: Planning for Peace of Mind

Chapter 9: Tools and Resources

Opening: Your Financial Toolkit

Worksheets and Templates

Monthly Budget Template

Net Worth Tracker

Goal Setting Worksheet

Digital Tools and Apps

Budgeting and Expense Tracking

Savings and Investments

Insurance and Emergency Planning

Debt Management

Activity: Building Your Digital Toolkit

How to Use These Tools

Conclusion: Empowering Your Partnership

Chapter 10: The Next Chapter

Opening: Looking Ahead Together

Key Takeaways

1. Marriage as a Partnership

2. Building a Strong Foundation

3. Adapting to Life's Changes

4. Embracing Technology

Your Next Steps

1. Revisit Your Marriage Business Plan

2. Plan Your Next Milestone

3. Keep the Conversation Going

A Personal Note

Closing Activity: Your Partnership Pledge

Final Thought

Appendix: Additional Resources

Tools for Financial Success

- Budgeting Apps

- Savings and Investment Platforms

- Debt Management Tools

Document Management

Recommended Reading

Personal Finance

- Relationships and Communication

Investing

Organizations for Assistance

- Military and First Responders

Financial Counseling

Nonprofit Resources

Glossary of Terms

Conclusion: Your Comprehensive Toolkit

Chapter 1: The Partnership of Marriage

Opening: Welcome to Your Next Adventure

"Congratulations! If you're here, you're either about to take, or have recently taken, one of the biggest steps in life: marriage. This book is here to help you do more than succeed—it's here to help you thrive."

Marriage is a beautiful adventure, but let's be real—it's also a partnership that requires some serious teamwork. Whether you're tackling finances, planning for the future, or just figuring out who's doing the dishes tonight, your success as a couple depends on how well you navigate life together.

My parents understood this better than anyone. As they wrote in their original book, *"A marriage is a contract between two individuals and represents the formation of a partnership. Like any small business, it requires combining assets, liabilities, and incomes to create a successful working system."* That idea is just as relevant today as it was in 2007, and it's the foundation of everything we'll talk about in this chapter.

Marriage as Your Joint Startup

Picture this: You and your partner are co-CEOs of a new company. The product? Your life together. The mission? Building a future filled with love, security, and maybe a little adventure. But like any business, your partnership needs a plan. You've got shared expenses, goals, and dreams to manage, and the choices you make now will shape your financial future.

In their original book, my parents had a simple way of framing this. They wrote, *"What remains after meeting your obligations is what businesses call 'profit,' and what couples call 'disposable income.' How that income is managed—whether saved, invested, or spent—often determines the financial health of the marriage."*

Their point? Managing your resources isn't just about money—it's about trust, communication, and building something bigger than yourselves.

The Marriage Business Plan

My parents introduced a framework they called the "Marriage Business Plan." It's straightforward, but it works:

1. **Combine Resources Wisely**: Lay it all out—income, debt, savings. Be honest and transparent with each other.
2. **Communicate Regularly**: Think of this like a monthly "board meeting" to review your budget, goals, and progress.

3. **Adapt as You Grow**: Life will throw curveballs—new jobs, kids, unexpected expenses. Adjust your plan together.

Let's take this one step further with a quick exercise:

- Sit down with your partner and answer this question: *What's one financial goal you both want to achieve this year?* Maybe it's paying off a credit card or saving for a vacation. Write it down and talk about how you'll get there.

Case Study: Emma and David

Let me tell you a quick story about Emma and David. When they got married, they were like most couples—excited, but a little clueless about money. Emma was a saver with spreadsheets for days, and David was a spender who loved to live in the moment. Naturally, this caused some friction.

One night, after a particularly tense argument about credit card bills, they decided to sit down and hash things out. They listed their income, debts, and expenses and created a simple plan:

- **50% of their income** would go to shared expenses like rent and groceries.
- **20% would go to savings**, with a goal of buying a home.
- **30% would be split** for fun spending and paying off David's student loans.

They also started using a budgeting app to keep things transparent. Over time, the tension faded, and they began working as a team. The lesson? Financial harmony isn't about being perfect—it's about being partners.

Modern Tools for Modern Couples

Back in 2007, couples had to rely on spreadsheets and calendars to manage their finances. Today, we've got tools that make it easier than ever to stay on track. Here are a few I recommend:

- **Honeydue**: A budgeting app designed for couples, perfect for tracking shared expenses.
- **Qapital**: Automates savings, so you're building your financial future without even thinking about it.
- **Mint**: A classic tool for creating budgets and keeping an eye on spending.

Pick the tool that feels right for you. The key isn't which app you use—it's how you use it to strengthen your partnership.

Your First Financial Goal

Let's wrap up this chapter with a challenge. Think about one financial goal you want to achieve as a couple this month. Maybe it's saving $100, setting up a joint account, or cutting back on takeout. Whatever it is, write it down, talk about it, and make a plan to tackle it together.

Marriage isn't about being perfect—it's about being a team. And like any great team, your strength comes from working together, communicating openly, and celebrating every little win.

What's Next

In the next chapter, we'll lay the groundwork for your Marriage Business Plan. From organizing your important documents to setting up joint accounts, we'll tackle the practical steps to building a strong financial foundation. Let's get started.

Chapter 2: Building Your Financial Foundation

Opening: The Blueprint for Success

"Every strong structure needs a solid foundation, and your marriage is no different."

If Chapter 1 was about understanding marriage as a partnership, this chapter is where we roll up our sleeves and get to work. We're going to lay the financial groundwork for your life together—everything from organizing your documents to setting up accounts and preparing for life's curveballs. Think of this as the blueprint for a secure and thriving partnership.

Here's a truth my parents shared in their original book: *"The success of a marriage often depends on the practical steps taken at the very beginning."* Whether you're newlyweds or simply looking to improve your financial life as a couple, this chapter will guide you through the essentials.

Legal and Practical Preparations

Organizing Your Important Documents

Marriage means combining more than just your lives—it also means combining your paperwork. Here's a checklist of documents every couple should have organized and accessible:

- <u>Marriage certificate</u>
- <u>Social Security cards</u>
- <u>Birth certificates</u>
- <u>Insurance policies (health, life, auto, property)</u>
- <u>Financial statements (bank accounts, investments, debts)</u>
- <u>Wills, living wills, and power of attorney</u>

Special Note for Military and First Responders:

If you're in the military, a first responder, or covered under a comprehensive employer-sponsored benefits package, some of this groundwork may already be laid out for you. Programs like TRICARE or employer-provided life insurance are incredible starting points, putting you a step closer to financial security. However, keep this in mind: if you transition out of these roles, you'll need to reassess your insurance and benefits to ensure no gaps arise.

** **Tip**: Use a digital vault like **Everplans** to securely store scanned copies of these documents. For physical copies, invest in a fireproof safe.

Setting Up Financial Systems

Joint Accounts: Yes, No, or Maybe?

One of the first big decisions couples face is whether to combine finances. There's no one-size-fits-all answer, but here's a breakdown of the options:

1. **Fully Joint Accounts**:
    - **Pros**: Simplifies budgeting and creates transparency.
    - **Cons**: Requires a lot of trust and communication.
2. **Fully Separate Accounts**:
    - **Pros**: Preserves individual autonomy.
    - **Cons**: Can complicate shared expenses.
3. **Hybrid Approach**:
    - **Pros**: Combines the best of both worlds—joint accounts for shared expenses, separate accounts for personal spending.
    - **Cons**: Requires a bit more effort to manage.

Emma and David's Hybrid Plan: After their rocky start, Emma and David decided on a hybrid system. They used a joint account for rent, utilities, and groceries while keeping separate accounts for hobbies and personal spending. To track everything, they used **Honeydue**, which automatically categorized their expenses.

Automating Your Finances

Automation is your best friend when it comes to managing money as a couple. Set up systems that work for you, like:

- **Automated bill payments**: Avoid late fees by scheduling recurring payments.

- **Savings triggers**: Use tools like **Qapital** to save a percentage of each paycheck or round up purchases.
- **Debt repayment plans**: Prioritize high-interest debts with apps like **Tally**, which creates custom repayment strategies.

Building Your Emergency Fund

Life happens—cars break down, jobs get lost, and unexpected bills pop up. That's why an emergency fund is non-negotiable.

The Rule of Thumb: Save 3–6 months' worth of essential expenses.

- **Starting Small**: Begin with a goal of $1,000. Once you hit that, aim higher.
- **Where to Keep It**: Use a high-yield savings account for quick access and better returns.

Special Note for Military and First Responders:
Many of your emergency needs may already be supported by programs like Servicemembers' Group Life Insurance (SGLI) or benefits from organizations like the VA or unions. These systems can provide a safety net, but be sure to plan for the future if you transition out of these roles.

Preparing for the Unexpected

Insurance Essentials

Insurance isn't the most exciting topic, but it's crucial for protecting your partnership. Here's what to consider:

- **Health Insurance**: If you're on separate plans,

compare costs and coverage to decide if combining makes sense.

- **Life Insurance**: A must if you're planning to have kids or buy a home. Start with term policies for affordability.

- **Renters or Homeowners Insurance**: Protects your home and belongings.

Special Note for Military and First Responders:
If you're covered by TRICARE, employer-sponsored health plans, or union-provided benefits, you're ahead of the curve. However, always keep an eye on transition plans to ensure you're covered in the long term.

Real-Life Example:

Maria and James had no idea their apartment wasn't covered for flood damage until a burst pipe left them with a $5,000 repair bill. Afterward, they upgraded their renters' insurance to include comprehensive coverage.

Activity: Your Financial Foundation Checklist

By the end of this chapter, you and your partner should:

- Have all your important documents organized (digitally or physically).
- Decide on your approach to joint accounts.
- Set up at least one automated savings or debt

repayment tool.
- Calculate your emergency fund goal and start building it.
- Review your insurance policies to fill any gaps.
- *If you're in the military or first responder roles, familiarize yourself with the benefits you already have and note any areas you'll need to address if you transition.*

Conclusion: A Strong Start

You've taken the first steps toward building a solid financial foundation. It might not seem glamorous, but trust me—it's these early preparations that set the stage for a partnership that can weather any storm.

In the next chapter, we'll take your foundation and build on it with a Marriage Business Plan—a clear roadmap for achieving your goals together. Let's keep the momentum going.

Chapter 3: Creating a Marriage Business Plan

Opening: Charting Your Path Together

"Every great partnership starts with a shared vision. Your marriage is no different."

By now, you've built the foundation: organized documents, set up financial systems, and begun preparing for the unexpected. Now, it's time to look ahead. This chapter is all about creating a roadmap—a Marriage Business Plan—that aligns your financial goals with your shared values and dreams.

Here's a principle my parents shared in their original book: *"A well-crafted financial plan for a marriage is akin to a business plan. It sets clear goals, defines shared responsibilities, and outlines steps to ensure long-term prosperity."* Today, we'll expand on that idea to help you and your partner set yourselves up for success.

Setting Shared Goals

A successful Marriage Business Plan starts with

understanding what you're working toward. Goals give you direction, purpose, and something to celebrate together.

Short-Term Goals (0–2 Years)

These are immediate priorities that build momentum:

- Creating an emergency fund.
- Paying off high-interest debt like credit cards.
- Saving for a honeymoon, a down payment, or another short-term goal.

Mid-Term Goals (2–10 Years)

These goals help you grow as a couple:

- Buying a home or upgrading your current living situation.
- Saving for a child's education or starting a family.
- Investing in shared experiences like travel or continuing education.

Long-Term Goals (10+ Years)

These goals secure your future:

- Building retirement savings through IRAs, 401(k)s, or investment accounts.
- Planning legacy goals, like funding charities or creating generational wealth.

Activity:

Take 10 minutes with your partner to write down 3–5 goals in each category. Discuss why these goals matter to you and what steps you'll need to take to achieve them.

Budgeting for Success

A good budget is like a map—it shows you where you are, where you want to go, and how to get there. Here's a simple framework:

The 50/30/20 Rule

This classic budgeting method divides your income into three categories:

1. **50% for Needs**: Rent, groceries, insurance, utilities.
2. **30% for Wants**: Hobbies, entertainment, travel.
3. **20% for Savings and Debt Repayment**: Emergency fund, retirement, paying off loans.

Modern Tools for Budgeting:

- **YNAB (You Need A Budget)**: Helps you allocate every dollar toward a specific purpose.
- **Goodbudget**: Mimics the envelope budgeting system in a digital format.
- **Mint**: Tracks spending and provides insights into your financial habits.

Incorporating Shared Values into Financial Goals

Marriage isn't just about financial security—it's about building a life that reflects your shared values. Here are a few ways to do that:

Faith-Based and Nonprofit Giving

Set aside a portion of your income for causes that matter to you. This could be a local charity, your place of worship, or a nonprofit focused on an issue you care about.

Investing in Shared Experiences

Use your budget to strengthen your bond. Whether it's a weekend getaway, a cooking class, or exploring a new city together, shared experiences can deepen your connection.

** **Tip**: Create a "Couple Bonding Fund" in your budget to save for meaningful activities that bring you closer.

Case Study: Maria and James

Maria and James are a couple in their early 30s. Maria is a corporate lawyer, and James works as a freelance graphic designer. They love each other deeply but quickly realized they had different approaches to money. Maria wanted a clear plan for the future, while James preferred a more relaxed, go-with-the-flow approach.

To bridge the gap, they created a Marriage Business Plan:

1. **Goals**: They identified three shared goals—building an emergency fund, saving for a home, and traveling once a year.

2. **Budget**: They used YNAB to allocate Maria's steady income to long-term goals while James' variable freelance income funded travel and other "fun" expenses.

3. **Regular Check-Ins**: They scheduled monthly "money dates" to review their progress and adjust their plan as needed.

The result? Less tension, more teamwork, and a clearer path to their dreams.

Military and First Responders: Leveraging Your Benefits

If you're in the military or a first responder, your Marriage Business Plan can leverage the incredible benefits already available to you:

- **Housing Assistance**: Programs like the VA Home Loan make buying a house more accessible.
- **Retirement Savings**: TSPs (Thrift Savings Plans) are an excellent way to build long-term wealth.
- **Health Coverage**: TRICARE and other plans provide a level of security many couples envy.

Important Note: As with earlier chapters, keep in mind that if you transition out of these roles, you'll need to reassess your benefits to ensure continued security.

Activity: Building Your Marriage Business Plan

Take an hour with your partner and complete the following:

1. Write down your short-, mid-, and long-term goals.
2. Draft a basic budget using the 50/30/20 rule.
3. Identify one shared value or cause to incorporate into your financial plan.
4. Set a date for your first "money meeting" to review and refine your plan.

Conclusion: From Vision to Reality

By creating a Marriage Business Plan, you're doing more than managing your money—you're creating a shared vision for your life together. The act of planning itself strengthens your bond, giving you clarity and confidence as a couple.

In the next chapter, we'll explore the day-to-day strategies for managing your finances, from choosing the right banking solutions to tackling debt and credit. Together, we'll turn your plan into action.

Chapter 4: Managing Everyday Finances

Opening: Turning Plans Into Action

"A good plan is only as strong as the actions you take to implement it. Managing your everyday finances is where your Marriage Business Plan truly comes to life."

Now that you've set your goals and built a foundation, it's time to tackle the day-to-day. From banking basics to debt management, this chapter is all about the practical tools and strategies you'll use to keep your finances on track.

Whether you're splitting bills, managing a budget, or dealing with unexpected expenses, the key to success is consistency. Remember: small, everyday decisions add up to big results over time.

Banking Basics: Choosing the Right Solutions

The right banking setup can simplify your financial life and reduce stress. Here's how to decide what works best for you as a couple:

Traditional vs. Online-Only Banks

- **Traditional Banks**:
    - Pros: In-person services, trusted reputations.
    - Cons: Lower interest rates on savings, higher fees.
- **Online-Only Banks**:
    - Pros: Higher interest rates, lower fees, and advanced tech features.
    - Cons: No physical branches for in-person help.

Pro Tip: If you're tech-savvy and prefer automation, online banks like Ally or Chime are great options. For couples who value face-to-face interactions, stick with a traditional bank.

Shared vs. Individual Accounts

Managing money as a couple doesn't mean you have to combine everything. Here are three approaches to consider:

1. **Joint Accounts**: Perfect for couples who want full transparency and simplicity.
2. **Separate Accounts**: Ideal for maintaining financial independence.
3. **Hybrid System**: Combine joint accounts for shared expenses (like rent and groceries) with individual accounts for personal spending.

** **Tip**: Use apps like **Honeydue** or **Splitwise** to track shared expenses if you're using separate accounts.

Credit and Debt Management

Understanding Credit Scores

Your credit score plays a huge role in your financial life, affecting everything from loans to insurance rates. Here's what you need to know:

- **Payment History (35%)**: Pay bills on time, every time.
- **Credit Utilization (30%)**: Keep balances below 30% of your credit limit.
- **Length of Credit History (15%)**: The longer, the better.

Pro Tip: Use tools like **Credit Karma** to monitor your score and get personalized tips for improvement.

Debt Repayment Strategies

Carrying debt isn't inherently bad, but managing it wisely is essential. Here are two popular repayment strategies:

1. **Snowball Method**: Pay off smaller debts first to build momentum.
2. **Avalanche Method**: Focus on debts with the highest interest rates for maximum savings.

Case Study: Sarah and Kyle were overwhelmed by credit card debt after their wedding. They chose the avalanche method, paying off the highest-interest card first while making minimum payments on the rest. After two years, they were debt-free and ready to start saving for a home.

Budgeting for Everyday Life

Simplifying Expense Tracking

Tracking your spending doesn't have to be a chore. AI-powered tools like **PocketGuard** or **Mint** can automatically categorize expenses and flag areas where you're overspending.

Activity: Use a budgeting app for one month and see where your money goes. Compare it to your budget and make adjustments.

Balancing Fixed and Variable Costs

Every couple's budget includes two types of expenses:

1. **Fixed Costs**: Rent, insurance, utilities—things that stay consistent.
2. **Variable Costs**: Groceries, entertainment, and subscriptions—things that fluctuate.

** **Tip**: Review your variable expenses regularly. Are there subscriptions or habits you can cut back on? Small changes can free up funds for your goals.

Managing Emergencies and Unexpected Costs

Health Crises

Medical emergencies can strain any couple's finances. Protect yourself by:

- Having comprehensive health insurance.
- Building a health-specific savings account for out-of-pocket costs.

Special Note for Military and First Responders: Programs like TRICARE or employer-sponsored plans often provide robust coverage. However, ensure you're prepared for unexpected gaps if you transition out of these roles.

Housing Costs

Whether you rent or own, housing costs can sneak up on you.

- Set aside 1–3% of your home's value annually for maintenance and repairs.
- If you rent, factor in potential increases at lease renewal.

Unexpected Expenses

Life happens—cars break down, appliances fail, and surprise bills show up. The best way to manage these is with your emergency fund. If that's not an option, consider:

- Negotiating payment plans.
- Using a low-interest credit option strategically.

Activity: Managing Day-to-Day Finances

By the end of this chapter, you and your partner should:

1. Choose a banking setup (joint, separate, or hybrid).
2. Monitor your credit scores and create a debt repayment plan if needed.
3. Track your expenses for a month and compare them to your budget.
4. Build or adjust your emergency fund to cover 3–6 months of essential costs.

Conclusion: Building Financial Resilience

Managing your finances isn't a one-time task—it's an ongoing process. The key is consistency and communication. With the tools and strategies in this chapter, you're ready to handle day-to-day challenges and keep your partnership strong.

In the next chapter, we'll look beyond the day-to-day and focus on building long-term security. From retirement planning to investing in your future, we'll help you lay the groundwork for lasting success.

Chapter 5: Building Long-Term Security

Opening: Planning for Tomorrow, Today

"Marriage isn't just about sharing the present; it's about building a future together."

You've tackled the day-to-day, but now it's time to think bigger. This chapter focuses on long-term financial security—ensuring that your marriage isn't just stable today but thriving for decades to come. From retirement planning to smart investments, this is where you lay the groundwork for the life you want to live, not just the one you're living now.

Long-term planning may not feel urgent, but it's one of the most important investments you can make in your partnership. As my parents wrote in their original book: *"Building security requires discipline, communication, and a shared vision for the future."* Today, we'll combine their wisdom with modern tools to make long-term planning easier than ever.

Retirement Planning for Couples

Start Early, Grow Steady

Retirement planning is one of the most significant financial challenges couples face, but the earlier you start, the easier it gets. Here's how to approach it:

1. **Maximize Employer Contributions**: If your employer offers a 401(k) match, take full advantage. It's essentially free money for your future.

2. **Explore IRAs**: Individual Retirement Accounts (IRAs) are a great way to supplement employer-sponsored plans.
   - **Traditional IRA**: Contributions are tax-deductible, but withdrawals are taxed.
   - **Roth IRA**: Contributions are taxed now, but withdrawals are tax-free later.

Special Note for Military and First Responders

If you're eligible for a Thrift Savings Plan (TSP), consider it a powerful retirement tool. With low fees and matching options, it's one of the best investments available. However, be sure to roll over funds into a civilian account if you transition out of service.

AI Assistance for Retirement Planning

AI tools can simplify retirement planning by helping you calculate contributions, project growth, and even adjust for inflation.

- **Betterment Retirement Planner**: Offers personalized insights and contribution suggestions.
- **Personal Capital**: Tracks retirement accounts and gives real-time projections for your financial goals.

Investing: Growing Your Wealth Together

The Power of Compounding

Every dollar you invest today has the potential to grow exponentially over time, thanks to compound interest. Even small, consistent contributions can lead to big results.

Diversification: Don't Put All Your Eggs in One Basket

Spread your investments across different asset classes:

- **Stocks**: Higher risk, higher potential return.
- **Bonds**: Lower risk, steady returns.
- **Mutual Funds and ETFs**: Great for beginners who want diversified portfolios.
- **Real Estate**: A long-term asset with rental income potential.

AI Tools for Investment Insights

- **Wealthfront**: A robo-advisor that builds and manages diversified portfolios.
- **Ziggma**: Offers AI-driven stock analysis to identify growth opportunities.

Activity: Your First Investment Plan

With your partner, decide on a monthly investment amount. Use a robo-advisor or speak with a financial planner to determine where to start. Even $50 a month can make a difference over time.

Protecting Your Partnership: Insurance Essentials

Key Types of Insurance

1. **Health Insurance**: Covers medical expenses, protecting your finances during health crises.
2. **Life Insurance**: Ensures your family's financial security if the unexpected happens.
    - **Term Policies**: Affordable and straightforward.
    - **Whole-Life Policies**: Combine insurance with a savings component.
3. **Disability Insurance**: Replaces income if illness or injury prevents you from working.
4. **Homeowners or Renters Insurance**: Protects your home and belongings.

Special Note for Military and First Responders

Servicemembers' Group Life Insurance (SGLI) and other employer-provided plans offer incredible value. However, evaluate whether supplemental coverage is necessary to fill gaps.

Case Study: Lisa and Mark's Holistic Approach

Lisa and Mark, in their early 50s, realized they hadn't done enough planning for their retirement or their children's future. They decided to take a proactive approach:

1. **Retirement Contributions**: Lisa maxed out her 401(k), and Mark opened a Roth IRA.

2. **College Savings**: They started a 529 plan for their youngest child.

3. **Insurance Upgrades**: They increased life insurance coverage and added long-term care insurance to prepare for eldercare needs.

4. **Tech Tools**: They used **Personal Capital** to track their progress and stay organized.

The result? Peace of mind and a clearer path toward their goals.

Legacy Planning: Creating a Lasting Impact

Wills and Trusts

- **Wills**: Specify how assets will be distributed and name guardians for minor children.
- **Trusts**: Avoid probate and provide detailed instructions for managing your estate.

Charitable Giving

If giving back is important to you, consider setting up a donor-advised fund or including charities in your will.

Activity: Planning Your Financial Future

1. Evaluate your retirement savings. Are you contributing enough to meet your long-term goals?

2. Discuss your investment strategy and make a plan to diversify your portfolio.

3. Review your insurance coverage for any gaps.

4. Create or update your will, ensuring it reflects your

current life stage.

Conclusion: Securing Your Future Together

Long-term financial security isn't just about numbers—it's about the peace of mind that comes from knowing you're building a stable future. By planning ahead, you're not just protecting yourselves—you're creating a legacy that reflects your shared values and dreams.

In the next chapter, we'll explore major life milestones—buying a home, starting a family, or launching a business—and how to prepare for them as a team. Let's keep building.

Chapter 6: Major Life Milestones

Opening: Preparing for the Big Moments

"Life is full of milestones, and each one brings its own set of opportunities and challenges."

Marriage is a journey marked by significant milestones—buying a home, starting a family, launching a business, or pursuing a career change. These moments are exciting, but they also require careful planning to navigate successfully. In this chapter, we'll guide you through the financial, emotional, and practical steps to prepare for life's big events.

As my parents emphasized in their original book: *"Planning ahead transforms life's challenges into opportunities."* By taking a proactive approach, you can enjoy these milestones without unnecessary stress.

Buying a Home Together

Financial Preparation

Buying a home is often the largest purchase a couple will make. To set yourselves up for success, start with these steps:

1. **Save for a Down Payment**: Aim for at least 10–20% of the home's value to avoid mortgage insurance and

lower your monthly payments.

2. **Get Pre-Approved**: Pre-approval shows sellers you're serious and gives you a clear budget.

3. **Check Your Credit Scores**: A strong credit score can secure better interest rates.

Hidden Costs of Homeownership

It's not just about the mortgage—be prepared for additional costs:

- **Property Taxes**: These vary by location and can increase over time.
- **Maintenance**: Budget 1–3% of the home's value annually for upkeep.
- **Insurance**: Ensure you have comprehensive homeowners insurance.

Special Note for Military and First Responders

If you're eligible, programs like the **VA Home Loan** offer significant advantages, including no down payment and lower interest rates. These benefits can make homeownership more accessible.

** **Tip**: Use tools like **Zillow** or **Rocket Mortgage** to research home prices and calculate monthly payments before you start house hunting.

Starting a Family

Financial Preparation for Parenthood

Expanding your family is one of life's most joyful milestones

—but it comes with significant costs. Here's how to prepare:

1. **Healthcare Costs**: Check your insurance coverage for maternity care, childbirth, or adoption.

2. **Childcare Expenses**: Plan for daycare, babysitters, or other childcare needs.

3. **Education Savings**: Open a **529 Plan** to start saving for your child's future education.

Activity: Calculate the estimated cost of childbirth or adoption in your area and create a savings plan.

Adoption and Fostering

If adoption or fostering is part of your plan, factor in agency fees, travel expenses, and potential legal costs. While fostering is often supported by state programs, you may need to budget for extracurricular activities or therapy.

Career Changes or Business Ventures

Planning for a Career Transition

A career change can be exciting but financially challenging. Here's how to prepare:

1. **Save 6–12 Months of Expenses**: Build a financial cushion before making the leap.

2. **Invest in Upskilling**: Platforms like **LinkedIn Learning** or **Coursera** can help you gain the skills needed for your next role.

3. **Explore Employer Benefits**: Some companies offer tuition reimbursement or career transition support.

Starting a Business

Launching a business with your partner—or supporting one another's entrepreneurial dreams—requires careful planning.

1. **Write a Business Plan**: Outline your goals, budget, and timeline.
2. **Separate Business and Personal Finances**: Open dedicated accounts to avoid confusion.
3. **Secure Funding**: Look into loans, savings, or investors to fund your startup.

** **Tip**: Use tools like **QuickBooks** for bookkeeping and **Bonsai** for contracts and invoicing.

Insurance: Beyond Basic Coverage

Every milestone brings new risks, and insurance is your safety net. Here's what to consider:

- **Life Insurance**: Adjust your coverage if you buy a home or start a family.
- **Disability Insurance**: Protects your income in case of illness or injury.
- **Umbrella Policies**: Offers additional liability protection beyond your standard policies.

Special Note for Military and First Responders

Employer-sponsored benefits may already cover many of these needs, but review your coverage annually to ensure it aligns with your goals.

Case Study: Maya and Chris

Maya and Chris had big dreams: buying a home, starting a family, and launching a business. To make it all work, they created a step-by-step plan:

1. **Homeownership**: They used a VA Home Loan to purchase their first house with no down payment.
2. **Starting a Family**: Maya and Chris opened a 529 Plan for their future child while researching childcare options.
3. **Launching a Business**: Chris transitioned to freelance work while Maya's stable income provided a safety net. They used **QuickBooks** to manage Chris's business finances.

The result? Maya and Chris achieved their milestones without sacrificing financial stability.

Activity: Your Milestone Checklist

For each milestone, discuss these questions with your partner:

1. What is our timeline for achieving this milestone?
2. What are the estimated costs, and how will we save for them?
3. What risks should we prepare for, and do we need additional insurance coverage?
4. What tools or resources can help us stay organized and on track?

Conclusion: Celebrating the Journey

Life's milestones are meant to be celebrated, but they're also opportunities to grow closer as a couple. By planning ahead and working as a team, you can approach each milestone with confidence and joy.

In the next chapter, we'll dive into adapting to challenges—navigating financial stress, managing job loss, and preparing for the unexpected. Let's keep moving forward.

Chapter 7: Adapting to Challenges

Opening: Strength Through Resilience

"Every partnership faces challenges, but how you navigate them together defines your success."

Life is unpredictable, and every couple will encounter bumps along the way. From financial stress to job loss, medical emergencies, or economic downturns, these moments can test your resilience as a team. This chapter is about preparing for and adapting to these challenges with a plan, a calm mindset, and clear communication.

As my parents wrote in their original book: *"Preparedness transforms setbacks into stepping stones."* With the right tools and strategies, you and your partner can tackle adversity together and come out stronger.

Navigating Financial Stress

Identifying Stress Triggers

Financial stress often arises from three main issues:

1. **Overspending**: Living beyond your means or succumbing to impulse purchases.
2. **Debt Accumulation**: High-interest loans and credit

card debt can feel overwhelming.

3. **Economic Pressures**: Inflation, job instability, or unexpected expenses.

** **Tip**: The first step to reducing stress is identifying the source. Take 15 minutes with your partner to pinpoint the root causes of your financial worries.

Creating a Financial Recovery Plan

When stress hits, a clear plan can help you regain control:

1. **Reassess Your Budget**: Focus on essentials and cut discretionary spending temporarily.
2. **Prioritize Debt Payments**: Target high-interest debt while maintaining minimum payments on others.
3. **Communicate Openly**: Check in regularly with your partner to adjust as needed.

Tools to Try:

- **PocketGuard**: Highlights areas where you can save.
- **Cleo**: Offers budgeting tips in a conversational, stress-free format.

Coping with Job Loss or Income Reductions

Preparing a Layoff Survival Plan

Job loss is a common stressor, but having a survival plan can make all the difference:

- **Emergency Fund**: Aim to cover 6–12 months of essential expenses.

- **Upskilling**: Invest in courses or certifications to broaden your job opportunities.
- **Networking**: Build and maintain professional connections.

** **Tip**: Explore gig platforms like **Upwork** or **Fiverr** to generate short-term income while you search for new opportunities.

Exploring New Income Streams

If your income is reduced, consider diversifying your earnings:

1. Freelancing or consulting in your area of expertise.
2. Online teaching or tutoring through platforms like **Skillshare** or **Teachable**.
3. Selling products or services on e-commerce sites like **Etsy** or **eBay**.

Managing Medical Emergencies

Planning for Healthcare Costs

A sudden medical issue can derail even the best-laid plans. Protect your finances by:

- Ensuring comprehensive health insurance coverage.
- Building a dedicated health emergency fund.

Special Note for Military and First Responders

Programs like TRICARE and employer-sponsored health plans often provide robust coverage. Ensure you understand your benefits and prepare for potential gaps if you transition out of these roles

Negotiating Medical Bills

If you face high medical costs, don't be afraid to negotiate:

1. Request an itemized bill and check for errors.
2. Speak with the billing department about payment plans or discounts.
3. Use tools like **GoodRx** for prescription savings.

Overcoming Economic Downturns

Adapting to Inflation

When costs rise, it's time to adjust:

- Switch to generic brands for groceries and household items.
- Review and renegotiate recurring bills like insurance or internet.

Investing During Recessions

While recessions can be intimidating, they also present opportunities:

- Consider **dollar-cost averaging**, investing consistently regardless of market conditions.
- Avoid emotional decisions—stay focused on long-term goals.

** **Tip**: Remember that markets recover. The key is patience and sticking to your plan.

Case Study: Anna and David

Anna and David faced a double challenge when David lost his job, and Anna required surgery after an unexpected accident. Here's how they adapted:

1. **Job Loss**: David turned to freelance work, using **Upwork** to supplement their income while searching for a full-time job.

2. **Medical Bills**: Anna negotiated her hospital bills, reducing them by 20%, and set up a zero-interest payment plan.

3. **Budget Adjustment**: They cut discretionary expenses and temporarily paused travel plans to rebuild their emergency fund.

4. **Emotional Resilience**: Weekly "check-ins" kept them focused and supportive of one another during the tough times.

The result? Anna and David not only overcame their challenges but also grew closer as a team.

Activity: Your Resilience Plan

With your partner, create a resilience plan for potential challenges:

1. Identify your top three financial risks (e.g., job loss, medical emergencies).

2. List the steps you can take to mitigate each risk (e.g., build an emergency fund, maintain insurance).

3. Agree on a check-in schedule to review your progress.

Conclusion: Facing Challenges as a Team

Every couple will face challenges, but it's how you respond that matters most. With preparation, communication, and a willingness to adapt, you can navigate even the toughest times and come out stronger.

In the next chapter, we'll focus on dissolution—planning for the unexpected realities of divorce or the death of a partner. These are difficult topics, but addressing them proactively ensures stability and peace of mind. Let's continue.

Chapter 8: Dissolution—Planning for the Unexpected

Opening: Preparing for Life's Difficult Transitions

"While every marriage begins with hope and optimism, life's uncertainties—whether through divorce or the death of a partner—can bring profound changes. Planning ahead can ensure stability during even the most challenging times."

This chapter addresses one of the most difficult aspects of life and marriage: dissolution. Whether it's a divorce or the passing of a partner, these moments are emotionally and financially complex. By taking proactive steps, you can protect your family, safeguard your assets, and ensure a smoother transition during a turbulent time.

Divorce: Legal and Financial Steps

The Importance of Professional Guidance

Navigating divorce requires a team of professionals to guide you through legal, financial, and tax-related decisions:

1. **Family Law Attorney**: Ensures your rights are protected during asset division and custody

arrangements.

2. **Certified Financial Planner (CFP)**: Provides insights on post-divorce budgeting and retirement savings.

3. **Certified Public Accountant (CPA)**: Helps address tax implications of property transfers and changes in filing status.

Understanding Asset Division

The way assets are divided depends on your location:

- **Community Property States**: Assets acquired during marriage are typically split 50/50.

- **Equitable Distribution States**: Assets are divided based on fairness, which doesn't always mean equally.

Activity: Create an inventory of all assets and debts to streamline discussions and negotiations.

Managing Shared Accounts and Debts

1. **Close Joint Accounts**: Protect yourself by separating finances early in the process.

2. **Refinance Loans**: Shift joint debts, like mortgages, into individual names where possible.

3. **Monitor Credit**: Keep an eye on your credit report to ensure there's no unauthorized activity on shared accounts.

** **Tip**: Mediation can be a less contentious and more cost-effective alternative to litigation for resolving financial disputes.

Planning for the Death of a Partner

Legal Documents to Prepare

1. **Wills**: Clearly outline how assets will be distributed and name guardians for any minor children.

2. **Trusts**: Help avoid probate and ensure assets are managed according to your wishes.

3. **Powers of Attorney**: Designate someone to handle financial and healthcare decisions if you're incapacitated.

Managing Life Insurance and Survivor Benefits

Life insurance provides crucial financial support for surviving partners and families.

- **Review Policies**: Ensure beneficiaries are updated regularly.
- **Understand Survivor Benefits**: Familiarize yourself with Social Security and employer-provided death benefits.

Special Note for Military and First Responders

Many military and first responder benefits, such as Servicemembers' Group Life Insurance (SGLI) or survivor pensions, provide significant support. However, ensure these plans are up to date and that your family knows how to access them.

Rebuilding Financial Stability After Dissolution

Adjusting Your Budget

- **Reassess Income and Expenses**: Create a new budget reflecting your current financial situation.

- **Focus on Essentials**: Prioritize housing, healthcare, and debt repayment.

Rebuilding Savings

- **Restart Emergency Fund Contributions**: Build 3–6 months of expenses as a buffer.
- **Retirement Savings**: If your retirement accounts were impacted, consider increasing contributions.

Exploring Resources

- **Legal Aid**: Organizations like Legal Aid Society provide support for those who need assistance.
- **Nonprofits**: Groups like the United Way connect individuals with housing, food, and financial counseling resources.

Case Study: Navigating Life's Transitions

Scenario 1: Divorce

Sarah and James divorced after 15 years of marriage. Here's how they managed the transition:

1. **Mediation**: They worked with a mediator to avoid costly litigation.
2. **Debt Reassignment**: James refinanced the mortgage into his name, taking full ownership of their house.
3. **Financial Counseling**: Sarah consulted a CFP to rebuild her retirement savings and plan for the future.

Scenario 2: Death of a Partner

Laura's husband, Mark, passed away unexpectedly. Because of their proactive planning, Laura was able to navigate the transition smoothly:

1. **Life Insurance Payout**: Laura used the funds to pay off their mortgage and create a college fund for their children.

2. **Trust Access**: Mark's trust allowed her immediate access to assets, avoiding a lengthy probate process.

3. **Community Support**: Laura leaned on grief counseling services and financial advisors to help her through the process.

Activity: Preparing for Dissolution

Take an hour with your partner to discuss and address the following:

1. Do we have up-to-date wills and trusts?
2. Are all beneficiary designations current?
3. Have we discussed life insurance and other survivor benefits?
4. Do we have an inventory of our assets and debts?

Conclusion: Planning for Peace of Mind

Dissolution is never easy, but preparation can make a profound difference. By addressing these issues now, you ensure that your family and finances are protected, no matter what life brings.

In the next chapter, we'll focus on tools and resources—

worksheets, templates, and digital tools to help you manage your finances with confidence. Let's bring it all together.

Chapter 9: Tools and Resources

Opening: Your Financial Toolkit

"The right tools make all the difference."

Throughout this book, we've explored the principles and practices of building a strong financial partnership. Now it's time to put those lessons into action. This chapter provides the worksheets, templates, and digital tools you need to manage your finances confidently and efficiently.

Whether you're organizing documents, creating a budget, or tracking your progress toward long-term goals, these resources are designed to make the process simple, clear, and effective.

Worksheets and Templates

Monthly Budget Template

This template helps you plan and track your monthly income and expenses.

Category	Projected ($)	Actual ($)
Income		
Salary		
Other Income		
Expenses		
Housing		
Utilities		
Transportation		
Groceries		
Debt Payments		
Insurance		
Savings/Investments		
Entertainment		
Miscellaneous		
Total		

** **Tip**: Use apps like **Mint** or **YNAB** to digitize your budget tracking for added convenience.

Net Worth Tracker

Keep track of your assets and liabilities with this simple worksheet.

Category	Value ($)	Notes
Assets		
Checking Accounts		
Savings Accounts		
Investments		
Home Value		
Vehicle Value		
Other Assets		
Liabilities		
Mortgage Balance		
Credit Card Debt		
Student Loans		
Other Liabilities		
Net Worth		(Assets - Liabilities)

Goal Setting Worksheet

Set and track your short-, mid-, and long-term goals.

Time Frame	Goal	Estimated Cost	Target Date	Progress (%)
Short-Term	Emergency Fund			
Mid-Term	Down Payment on Home			
Long-Term	Retirement Savings			

Activity: Sit with your partner and fill out this worksheet together. Revisit it every three months to track progress and make adjustments.

Digital Tools and Apps

Budgeting and Expense Tracking

- **YNAB (You Need A Budget)**: Helps you allocate every dollar and plan for future expenses.
- **Mint**: Tracks spending, categorizes expenses, and provides budgeting insights.
- **Honeydue**: Specifically designed for couples to manage shared expenses and bills.

Savings and Investments

- **Qapital**: Automates savings by rounding up purchases or setting specific rules.
- **Wealthfront**: A robo-advisor for building diversified investment portfolios.
- **Acorns**: Helps you start investing with spare change.

Insurance and Emergency Planning

- **Policygenius**: Compares insurance policies to find the best coverage for your needs.
- **Everplans**: A digital vault for storing critical documents and sharing them with trusted contacts.

Debt Management

- **Tally**: Consolidates and automates credit card debt payments to reduce interest.
- **Credit Karma**: Tracks credit scores and provides insights for improving them.

Activity: Building Your Digital Toolkit

1. Choose one app for budgeting, one for savings, and

one for debt management.

2. Set them up together and explore their features.

3. Schedule a "tech check-in" to review your tools and their impact after three months.

How to Use These Tools

1. **Simplify Your Workflow**: Use digital tools to automate tasks like bill payments, savings contributions, and debt repayment.

2. **Stay Consistent**: Revisit your worksheets and apps regularly to ensure you're on track.

3. **Adjust as Needed**: Life changes—so should your tools and plans. Reassess your system as your needs evolve.

** **Tip: Create a "Financial Dashboard"**

Compile all your tools and templates in one place—a shared Google Drive folder, a physical binder, or an app like Evernote. This makes it easy to access everything you need at a glance.

Conclusion: Empowering Your Partnership

These tools and resources are designed to help you take control of your finances and build a thriving partnership. The key is to start small, stay consistent, and communicate openly with your partner. With the right tools in hand, you're equipped to tackle any challenge and achieve your shared dreams.

In the final chapter, we'll wrap up with a reflection on everything we've covered and how to carry these lessons forward into a thriving future together.

Chapter 10: The Next Chapter

Opening: Looking Ahead Together

"Marriage is a journey, and every step you take together strengthens your partnership."

As we come to the end of this book, it's time to reflect on everything you've learned and look ahead to the future you're building together. Marriage is a dynamic partnership—it evolves as you grow, face challenges, and achieve milestones. The lessons and tools in this book are meant to guide you not just today, but for years to come.

Key Takeaways

1. Marriage as a Partnership

From the beginning, we've framed marriage as more than a romantic union. It's a partnership that requires shared goals, open communication, and thoughtful planning. By treating your marriage like a well-run business, you can navigate challenges and seize opportunities with confidence.

2. Building a Strong Foundation

Your foundation—organized documents, financial systems, and emergency planning—is the bedrock of your partnership.

Revisit these systems regularly to ensure they continue to serve you as your needs evolve.

3. Adapting to Life's Changes

Whether it's financial stress, a job loss, or major life milestones, flexibility is key. Life rarely goes exactly as planned, but with the tools and strategies in this book, you're equipped to adapt and thrive.

4. Embracing Technology

The modern tools we've discussed—from budgeting apps to AI-powered savings platforms—simplify financial management and make collaboration easier. Don't be afraid to experiment with new technologies to find what works best for you.

Your Next Steps

1. Revisit Your Marriage Business Plan

Take time with your partner to review your goals, budget, and financial systems. Ask yourselves:

- Are we on track with our goals?
- Do we need to adjust anything to reflect changes in our lives?

2. Plan Your Next Milestone

What's the next big step in your journey? Whether it's buying a home, starting a family, or launching a business, use the tools in this book to prepare and plan.

3. Keep the Conversation Going

Schedule regular check-ins to discuss your finances, goals, and overall partnership. Open communication is the cornerstone of a successful marriage.

A Personal Note

This book has been a deeply personal project for me, not just because of my own experiences, but because it builds on the incredible work of my parents. Their wisdom, combined with the lessons I've learned over the years, has shaped every chapter of this book. My hope is that these insights will guide you and your partner as you navigate your own journey.

Remember: no marriage is perfect, and every partnership has its ups and downs. What matters most is your commitment to working together, supporting each other, and growing as a team.

Closing Activity: Your Partnership Pledge

Take a moment with your partner to create a pledge for your marriage. It can be as simple or detailed as you like. Here's a starting point:

"We pledge to communicate openly, plan thoughtfully, and support each other through every challenge and triumph. Together, we will build a partnership that reflects our values, achieves our dreams, and grows stronger with every step we take."

Write it down, sign it, and revisit it whenever you need a reminder of the commitment you've made to each other.

Final Thought

Your journey as a couple is uniquely yours. This book is just the beginning of what you can achieve together. As you move forward, remember to celebrate your wins, learn from your challenges, and embrace the incredible adventure of building a life together.

Thank you for letting this book be part of your journey. Here's to your partnership, your dreams, and your future — together.

Appendix: Additional Resources

Tools for Financial Success

Budgeting Apps

- **YNAB (You Need A Budget)**: Helps allocate every dollar toward a purpose.
- **Mint**: Tracks spending and provides insights into your financial habits.
- **Honeydue**: Ideal for couples managing shared expenses.

Savings and Investment Platforms

- **Qapital**: Automates savings with customizable rules.
- **Wealthfront**: A robo-advisor for diversified investing.
- **Acorns**: Makes investing easy with round-ups from everyday purchases.

Debt Management Tools

- **Tally**: Consolidates and automates credit card debt payments.
- **Credit Karma**: Tracks credit scores and offers tips for improvement.

Document Management

- **Everplans**: Securely stores essential documents and allows sharing with trusted contacts.

Recommended Reading

Personal Finance

- *The Total Money Makeover* by Dave Ramsey
- *I Will Teach You to Be Rich* by Ramit Sethi

Relationships and Communication

- *The 5 Love Languages* by Gary Chapman
- *Crucial Conversations: Tools for Talking When Stakes Are High* by Patterson, Grenny, et al.

Investing

- *The Simple Path to Wealth* by JL Collins
- *A Random Walk Down Wall Street* by Burton Malkiel

Organizations for Assistance

Military and First Responders

- **USO**: Resources for active-duty military families.
- **Code Green Campaign**: Mental health support for first responders.

Financial Counseling

- **National Foundation for Credit Counseling (NFCC)**: Nonprofit financial advice.
- **Consumer Financial Protection Bureau (CFPB)**: Free tools and advice for managing money.

Nonprofit Resources

- **United Way**: Connects individuals with local financial and social services.
- **Habitat for Humanity**: Affordable housing programs.

Glossary of Terms

A

- **Account**: A financial arrangement with a bank or institution to hold and manage your money.
- **Asset**: Anything of value owned by an individual or couple, such as a home, car, or investments.

B

- **Budget**: A plan for managing income and expenses.
- **Buy Now, Pay Later**: A payment method that allows purchases to be paid off in installments over time.

C

- **Community Property**: A legal system where assets acquired during marriage are owned equally by both spouses.
- **Credit Score**: A numerical representation of your creditworthiness based on your financial history.

D

- **Debt**: Money owed to lenders, such as credit card balances, student loans, or mortgages.
- **Diversification**: Spreading investments across different asset types to reduce risk.

E

- **Emergency Fund**: Savings set aside for unexpected expenses or financial hardships.
- **Equitable Distribution**: A legal principle for dividing

marital assets based on fairness rather than a strict 50/50 split.

I

- **Income**: Money received from wages, investments, or other sources.
- **Investment**: Allocating money with the expectation of earning a return over time.

J

- **Joint Account**: A bank account shared by two or more individuals, often used for shared expenses.

L

- **Liability**: A financial obligation or debt owed to another party.
- **Life Insurance**: A policy providing financial support to beneficiaries upon the policyholder's death.

M

- **Mortgage**: A loan used to purchase real estate, typically repaid over many years.

R

- **Retirement Account**: A financial account, such as a 401(k) or IRA, designed to grow savings for retirement.

S

- **Savings Account**: A bank account used to store money

for short- or long-term goals.
- **Stock**: A share of ownership in a company, representing a claim on its assets and earnings.

T

- **Trust**: A legal arrangement for managing assets, often used to avoid probate or ensure inheritance distribution.
- **Thrift Savings Plan (TSP)**: A retirement savings plan for federal employees and military personnel.

W

- **Will**: A legal document specifying how a person's assets should be distributed after their death.

Conclusion: Your Comprehensive Toolkit

The tools, resources, and definitions in this appendix are here to simplify your journey and help you take control of your financial partnership. Revisit these as often as needed, and use them as a springboard for continuous growth and success.

Acknowledgement

I would like to express my deepest gratitude to my husband, John M. Peifer, whose unwavering love, support, and encouragement have been my guiding light throughout the journey of completing this book. Since we married on April 20, 2015, John has been my greatest champion, offering both emotional and practical support when it was needed most. Without his belief in me and in this project, I would not have been able to bring this work to fruition. This book is as much his achievement as it is mine, and I am forever grateful for his partnership in both life and work.

About The Author

Scott J. Spivey

Scott J. Spivey is a financial expert, author, and advocate for marriage as a partnership that combines both love and practicality. Building upon the foundational work of his parents, Dr. C. Willard Spivey, Jr. and Karon Spivey, Scott has dedicated his career to helping couples navigate the often-overlooked financial aspects of their relationships. His deep understanding of personal finance, along with his firsthand experiences in observing his parents' 60+ years of partnership, has shaped his approach to financial guidance.

With a passion for empowering couples to create secure, thriving futures together, Scott has reimagined The Business Side of Marriage in this updated edition. Combining time-tested principles with the latest tools and technologies, Scott's advice is grounded in practical strategies for achieving long-term success, regardless of the challenges that life may bring. He believes that the key to a strong partnership lies in shared goals, transparent communication, and thoughtful planning.

Scott's writing reflects his own values of resilience, teamwork, and mutual support—principles that have guided both his personal life and his professional career. As an advocate for modern marriage, Scott's work continues to inspire couples to build not just a financial foundation, but a legacy of love and success together.

Case Study: Mike and Victoria Smith—Building a Faith-Based Financial Future

Introduction

Mike and Victoria Smith, both hardworking and dedicated to building a strong foundation for their family, are navigating the complexities of balancing careers, finances, and their desire to provide a faith-based upbringing for their future children. Married in 2025, Mike, a 25-year-old state police officer, and Victoria, a 22-year-old assistant manager in a local restaurant, have set ambitious goals for their lives. Their priorities include raising two children in a private, faith-based school environment, retiring by 55, and enjoying quality beachside vacations as a family.

Chapter 1: Marriage As A Partnership

The Early Years: Establishing a Foundation

Mike and Victoria's journey together began when they married young, both motivated by faith, ambition, and love. Mike had been in the state police department for a couple of years, while Victoria had recently been promoted to assistant manager at the restaurant. Their shared values—particularly their strong commitment to their faith—serve as a compass for their financial and life decisions.

Their marriage, much like a business partnership, required them to merge their financial resources, create shared goals, and build a strong foundation. Recognizing the importance of transparency and communication, they decided to openly discuss their financial situation and future goals early on.

Their _**Marriage Business Plan**_ focused on a few key objectives:
- Saving for their future children's education at a private, faith-based school.
- Ensuring a comfortable retirement by age 55.
- Managing their current finances with a joint checking account while maintaining individual accounts for personal spending.

Victoria's job provides a steady income, while Mike's work as a police officer requires shift flexibility and, often, overtime. They made a conscious decision to **budget 20% of their combined income** for savings, prioritizing their **emergency fund**, future education expenses, and retirement.

Chapter 2: Setting Shared Goals

Planning for Children and Their Education

Mike and Victoria always knew they wanted to raise children in a faith-based environment. Their vision for their children's education was clear: they planned to send them to a private Christian school for both primary and secondary education. They understand that this will require careful financial planning and the setting aside of substantial funds.

The cost of private school tuition is a significant consideration in their budget. Research shows that private schools can range from $5,000 to $15,000 per year, depending on the school and grade level. With plans to have two children, they estimate a total of $300,000 to $600,000 in education costs over the next 15 years.

Budgeting and Saving for Education:
- Mike and Victoria aim to start saving as soon as possible by setting up a **529 College Savings Plan**, which allows them to put aside tax-advantaged funds specifically for education.
- They commit to saving $500 per month towards this fund, increasing the amount as their incomes grow over the years.

Chapter 3: Managing Everyday Finances

Income, Expenses, and Shared Goals

Mike and Victoria's income comes from two primary sources:
- *Mike's Salary:* As a state police officer, Mike's salary is supplemented by occasional overtime pay. However, he also

incurs costs like maintaining his police cruiser, which is provided by the department but requires regular upkeep.
- *Victoria's Salary:* As an assistant manager, Victoria has a steady income with potential bonuses based on restaurant performance.

Since they share a private car but Mike uses his cruiser during the day, their transportation costs are minimal. They decided to keep their shared expenses for gas, insurance, and maintenance to a reasonable level by budgeting $200 per month for transportation-related costs.

Budgeting Framework:
Mike and Victoria adopted the *50/30/20 rule* for their budget:
- *50% Needs:* Housing, utilities, groceries, health insurance, transportation.
- *30% Wants:* Dining out, entertainment, vacations.
- *20% Savings and Debt Repayment:* Contributions to emergency fund, retirement accounts, and education savings.

They created a detailed *monthly budget* that helps them track their spending. They found that by using digital tools like Mint and Honeydue, they could easily monitor their shared and individual expenses, reducing stress and avoiding financial surprises.

Chapter 4: Building Long-Term Security

Retirement Planning: Aiming for Early Retirement

One of the Smiths' long-term goals is to retire at the age of 55. This ambitious goal requires careful planning and discipline in saving and investing. Mike and Victoria want to ensure they have enough funds to cover their living expenses during retirement and maintain their lifestyle, including vacations.

Retirement Strategy:
- Mike and Victoria began contributing to employer-sponsored **401(k) plans** and opened a **Roth IRA** for additional retirement savings. They aim to contribute at least **15% of their combined income** annually toward retirement.
- Additionally, they are focusing on *investing in index funds* to grow their wealth steadily over time, allowing the power of compound interest to work in their favor.

Emergency Fund:
Mike and Victoria's goal is to have an emergency fund that covers at least six months of their living expenses. They currently have $15,000 saved and are contributing $500 monthly to increase this amount.

Chapter 5: Preparing For Major Life Milestones

Milestones: Building a Home and Starting a Family

Mike and Victoria dream of buying a house and raising their children in a stable, loving environment. They know that buying a home and preparing for parenthood will require significant financial resources.

Buying a Home:
They are currently renting, but their goal is to purchase a home in the next five years. To prepare for this, they are saving for a **down payment** by setting aside $1,000 per month. They also plan to use a **VA loan**, which will allow them to avoid a down payment and secure favorable mortgage terms due to Mike's position in the police force.

Starting a Family:
With plans to have two children, Mike and Victoria are making sure their budget includes expenses for childcare, health insurance, and potential medical costs related to pregnancy and childbirth. They are setting aside *$1,500 per month* into a **dedicated savings account** to cover these costs.

Chapter 6: Adapting To Challenges

Handling Financial Stress and Unexpected Costs

Like many couples, Mike and Victoria have faced challenges that required resilience and teamwork. For example, when Victoria's restaurant temporarily cut back hours due to economic downturns, they adjusted their budget by focusing on essential spending and dipping into their emergency fund.

Preparing for the Unexpected:
Mike and Victoria have learned the importance of having an emergency plan in place. They have a **financial recovery strategy** for handling unexpected expenses, including setting aside funds for medical emergencies, car repairs, and

other unforeseen costs.

Chapter 7: The Dissolution Plan

Preparing for Life's Unexpected Transitions

While it may seem counterintuitive to think about dissolution so early in their marriage, Mike and Victoria have set up key legal and financial safeguards to protect themselves and their future children.

They have:
- **Updated Wills** to ensure their children are taken care of in case of their passing.
- **Life Insurance** policies to protect their family financially.
- **Powers of Attorney** to manage healthcare and financial decisions should either partner become incapacitated.

Conclusion

Mike and Victoria Smith are well on their way to building a stable and prosperous future together. By prioritizing their shared values, setting clear goals, and working together to create a comprehensive financial plan, they are positioning themselves for success in both their marriage and their finances.

Through diligent saving, careful budgeting, and the use of modern tools and strategies, they will be able to achieve their dreams of a faith-based education for their children, an early retirement at 55, and the ability to enjoy many beachside vacations along the way.

Made in the USA
Columbia, SC
23 March 2025